Police Officer

Copyright © QED Publishing 2009

First published in the UK in 2009 by
QED Publishing
A Quarto Group company
226 City Road
London EC1V 2TT

www.qed-publishing.co.uk

A catalogue record for this book is available
from the British Library.

ISBN 978 1 84835 158 5

Printed and bound in China

Author Amanda Askew
Designer and Illustrator Andrew Crowson
Consultants Shirley Bickler and Tracey Dils

Publisher Steve Evans
Creative Director Zeta Davies
Managing Editor Amanda Askew

Words in bold are
explained in the
glossary on page 24.

Police Officer

Amanda Askew
Andrew Crowson

QED
QED Publishing

Meet Anita. She is a police officer. She helps to **prevent crime** and keep people safe.

At 7 o'clock, Anita arrives at the **police station** and changes into her **uniform**.

Anita's hat, suit and badge make up her uniform. Her uniform lets people know that she is a police officer.

In the morning, the
officers have a meeting
with the **sergeant**.

Anita goes out **on patrol**
in the town.

The **traffic** is very busy outside
the local school and the children
cannot cross the road.

Anita stands in the road and holds
up her hand to stop the cars.

"I don't want you to be late for school!"
"Thanks Officer."

Then, Anita gets a message on her radio. Some computer games have been stolen from a store on Hall Street.

When Anita arrives,
the shopkeeper
is waiting outside.

"Officer, two boys stole
some computer games."
"Please start from the beginning
and tell me what happened."

The shopkeeper tells Anita that one boy asked him for help, while the other boy put the computer games up his t-shirt. When the shopkeeper saw this, the boys ran away.

12

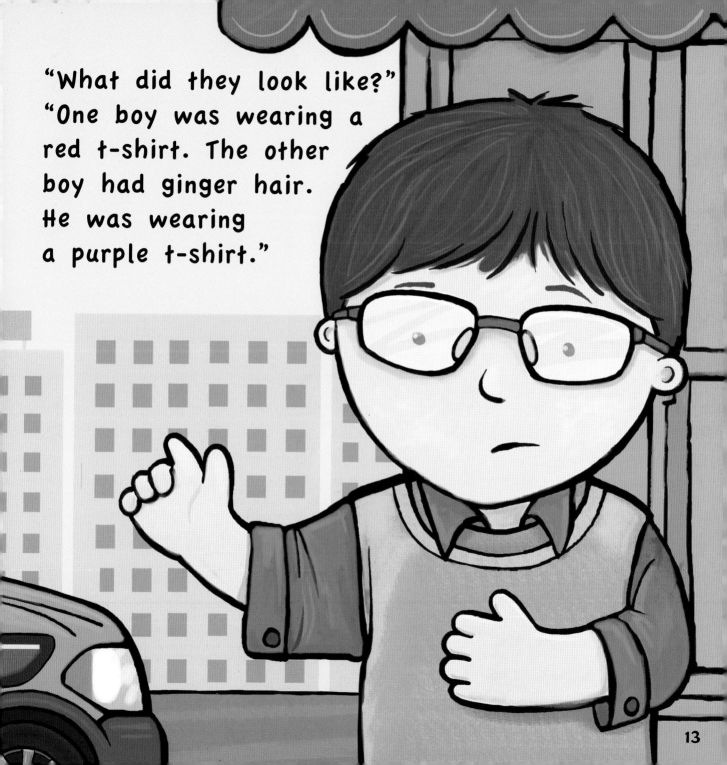

"What did they look like?"
"One boy was wearing a red t-shirt. The other boy had ginger hair. He was wearing a purple t-shirt."

13

Back at the station, Anita phones the local school to see if anyone is absent today.

"Thomas and Ross Green aren't at school."
"Thanks, Miss Nakata. I'll go round and see their parents."

On Anita's way to the Green's home, the car in front of her doesn't stop when the traffic lights turn red.

Anita turns on her **siren** and follows the car. This tells the driver to stop.

"Why didn't you stop at the traffic lights?"
"I'm sorry, Officer. I was trying to swat a wasp. I didn't see the lights turn red."

"You could have caused an **accident**. Next time, pull over to the side of the road and stop the car first."

Outside the boys' house, Anita sees Ross and Thomas.

"Thomas! Ross! I think we need to have a chat, don't you? Let's go inside and speak to your parents."

Anita talks to the boys and their parents. The boys admit that they took the games.

"**Stealing** is wrong. People can go to **jail** for it. Instead, we'll take the games back to the store and tell the owner that you're sorry."

"Yes, Officer. We are very sorry. We'll never do it again."

23

Glossary

Accident A car crash.

Jail A place where people who break the law are kept.

On patrol When a police officer walks around to check there is no crime.

Police station A place where police officers work.

Prevent crime To stop someone doing something that is against the law.

Radio Equipment that is used to send spoken messages.

Sergeant An important person in the police force.

Siren Equipment that makes a loud warning noise.

Stealing Taking something that isn't yours.

Traffic Cars, buses and other vehicles on the road.

Uniform A type of clothing worn by police officers.